SEE and SAY

Nursery Rhymes

Jaslynn Anderson

Dedication

This book is dedicated to infants, toddlers, pre-k, kindergarteners, and elementary children around the world and their families, guardians, close friends, and teachers.

123, I am Happy.

Bad, bad, bad, I am really sad.

Blue, blue, blue. My love is true.

Think, think, think. your eyes blink.

Round and around, I can make a sound.

Don't be mean, trees are green.

Who, who, who, I see you.

Down, down, down, bears are brown.

4…5…6, I see sticks.

Red, red, red, a hat for your head.

Pop, pop, pop, I'm on top.

This and that, feed a cat.

Color me blue, who are you?

Blocks, blocks, blocks, I have rocks in my socks.

Rope, rope, rope, a bar of soap.

Hot, hot, hot, potatoes in a pot.

Wow, wow, wow, away we go.

Drive, drive, drive, let's say bye.

Come in, come out, I see a pout.

Smear, smear, smear, I see a tear.

Run, run, run. Let's have fun.

Carry, carry, carry, I see a ferry.

Rows, rows, rows, look at your toes.

7…8…9, your love is mine.

Up and down, make a sound.

Well, well, well, what's that smell?

Me, me, me, there is a tree.

Hello, hello, hello, the sun is yellow.

Yarn, yarn, yarn, animals in the barn

…10, I can win.

About the Author

Jaslynn is a commencing writer who grew up in California where she started her writing journey. She has a great desire to help families embark on teaching and learning all over the world.

She hopes that everyone enjoys this exciting and vibrant book, that she wrote with a vision to enable parents and families to teach their little ones at an early age how to begin to read.